DEC   2001

DATE DUE

Volcanoes of the World ™

Krakatoa
History's Loudest Volcano

Kathy Furgang

The Rosen Publishing Group's
PowerKids Press ™
New York

For Beulah

Published in 2001 by The Rosen Publishing Group, Inc.
29 East 21st Street, New York, NY 10010

First Edition

Series and Book Design: Michael Caroleo

Photo Credits: pp. 1, 12 © Sergio Dorantes/CORBIS; p. 4 © North Wind; p. 7 (illustration) by Michael Caroleo; p. 8 © Ralph White/CORBIS; pp. 11, 16 © CORBIS; p. 15 © Hirz/Archive Photo; p. 19 © International Stock; p. 20 © Jack Fields/CORBIS.

Furgang, Kathy.
     Mt. Krakatoa : history's loudest volcano / by Kathy Furgang.—1st ed.
        p. cm.— (Volcanoes of the world)
     Includes index.
     ISBN 0-8239-5662-8 (alk. paper)
     1. Krakatoa (Indonesia)—Juvenile literature. 2. Volcanoes—Indonesia—Juvenile literature. [1. Krakatoa (Indonesia) 2. Volcanoes.] I. Title: Mount Krakatoa. II. Title.

QE523.K73 F87 2000
551.21'09598—dc21   00-028594

Manufactured in the United States of America

Contents

1 Krakatoa   5

2 Where Does a Volcano Come From?   6

3 Forming Under Water   9

4 Making an Island   10

5 Trouble Comes to Krakatoa   13

6 Did You Hear That?   14

7 A Changing Island   17

8 Water, Water Everywhere   18

9 Krakatoa Sunsets   21

10 Child of Krakatoa   22

Glossary   23

Index   24

Web Sites   24

Krakatoa had been silent and peaceful, as in this photograph, for more than 200 years before the eruption of 1883.

Krakatoa

Imagine a country in the middle of the ocean that is made up of more than 13,500 tiny islands. This is what the country of Indonesia is like. Indonesia is in the Pacific Ocean between Asia and Australia. About half of these islands do not have people living on them. Many of the islands of Indonesia are made up of dangerous volcanoes. A volcano is a hill or mountain that is formed when hot liquid from inside Earth breaks through the surface. A volcano in Indonesia, called Krakatoa, is one of the most famous volcanoes in the world. In 1883, Krakatoa **erupted**. The explosion was heard thousands of miles (km) away, as far away as Australia and Japan.

5

Where Does a Volcano Come From?

Our Earth is made up of three layers. The top part is called the **crust**. This is the outer layer were we live. Miles (km) below the crust is a layer called the **mantle**. The mantle is made up of solid rock and a hot liquid rock called **magma**. The very center of Earth is called the **core**. The outer core is made mostly of liquid iron. The inner core is solid iron and other elements. A volcano happens when hot magma from Earth's mantle shoots through a break in the crust and reaches to the surface of Earth. Magma that reaches the surface of Earth is called **lava.**

Crust

Mantle

Core

The part of the mantle that is closest to the crust has a temperature of around 1,600 degrees Fahrenheit (870 degrees C). The center of the core is around 11,000 degrees Fahrenheit (6,100 degrees C)!

This is an image of a submarine volcano erupting under the ocean.

Forming Under Water

Sometimes volcanoes begin on the ocean floor. A volcano that begins like this is called a **submarine volcano**. There are thousands of submarine volcanoes on Earth. They are so far under water that we usually cannot tell when they are erupting. Some submarine volcanoes erupt so many times that the lava from the eruptions begins to pile up. If enough lava piles up, the volcano will reach up out of the ocean and become an island. This is what happened to form many of the islands in Indonesia. Krakatoa is one of these volcanic islands that began on the ocean floor.

Making an Island

Thousands of years ago, magma broke through the crust of Earth under the ocean and began to pile up. Each time there was an eruption under the ocean, another layer of lava was added on top of the old one. The volcano being formed by the lava kept getting taller, until it reached out of the ocean and made its own volcanic island.

In 416 A.D., an eruption broke this volcanic island into several smaller pieces. One of these pieces was Krakatoa. Each time Krakatoa erupted, another layer of lava made the island bigger. By 1883, Krakatoa was a volcanic island that measured 2.5 miles (4 km) long and 5.6 miles (9 km) wide.

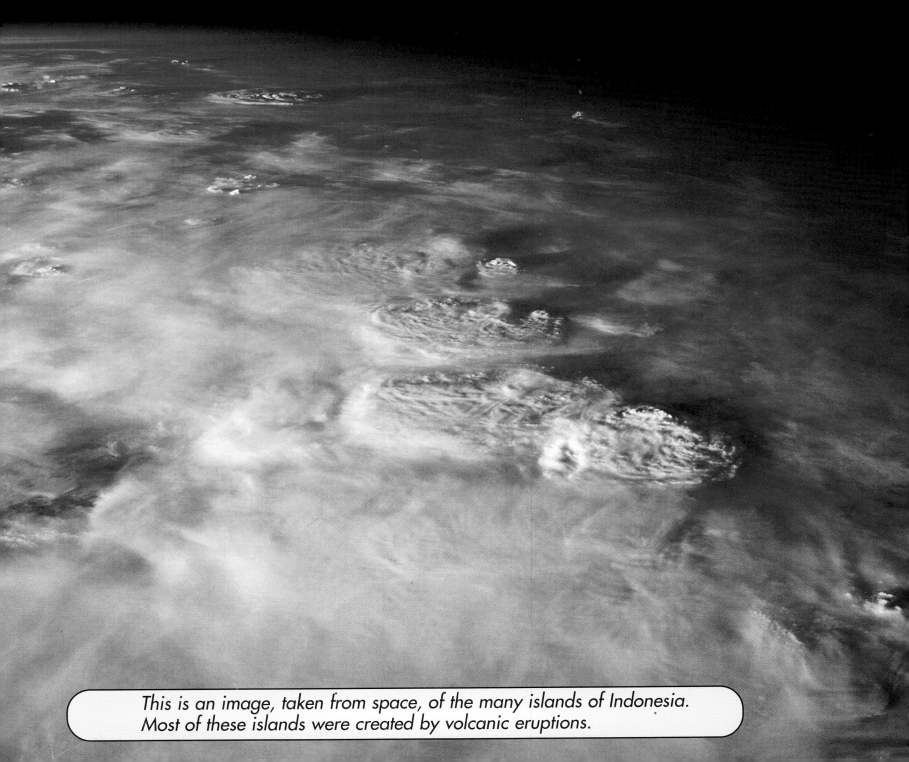

This is an image, taken from space, of the many islands of Indonesia.
Most of these islands were created by volcanic eruptions.

This is Mount Krakatoa with dark smoke rising out of it. Small eruptions of gas and smoke can be warnings that a larger eruption is on the way.

Trouble Comes to Krakatoa

Krakatoa began erupting on August 26, 1883, and continued to erupt for 100 days. This eruption was the worst eruption in the history of Krakatoa. Some volcanoes give warnings before they erupt. One of the signs that a volcano may erupt is an **earthquake**. These movements and shakes in the ground show that the **plates** are moving and that an eruption may soon follow. Many strong earthquakes happened in the area around Krakatoa between 1877 and 1883. Then in August of 1883, small eruptions began happening on the island.

13

Did You Hear That?

Imagine the loudest noise ever heard. That's how many people described the sound of Krakatoa erupting in 1883! The eruption began at lunchtime on Sunday, August 26th. The worst, and loudest, part of the eruption happened on Monday morning. Giant rocks blasted off the mountain into tiny pieces. Thick smoke and dust traveled miles (km) into the sky. More than half the island was blown apart. The eruption turned the sky black with **ash**. It also caused lightning, wind, and huge waves in the ocean. Dust, ash, and **gases** in the air made it hard for people to breathe.

This is a photo of Krakatoa erupting and sending thick black smoke out over the Pacific Ocean in August of 1883.

This is an image of the caldera that was formed by the eruption of Krakatoa.

A Changing Island

After the furious eruptions on Sunday, August 26, and Monday, August 27, 1883, the island of Krakatoa looked very different. The 18-square-mile (46.6-sq-km) island was now a six-square-mile (15.5-sq-km) island. Large pieces of lava were floating in the ocean after being blown off the mountain. This made traveling dangerous for sailing ships. They used the area around Krakatoa to bring goods from Europe to Asia. Most of the volcano's smoke had come out of a 600-foot **crater** on the island. The crater had been formed hundreds of years earlier when part of the volcano caved in on itself. After the 1883 eruption, the crater was even bigger than before. A crater formed by a volcano is called a **caldera**.

Water, Water Everywhere

No one lived on Krakatoa. For people who lived on islands around Krakatoa, however, the volcano was far more than a noisy explosion of rock. Thirty-six thousand people died from Krakatoa's eruption. Most of these people died by drowning. Since Krakatoa was so near to the ocean, many of the eruptions from the volcano happened under the water. During the eruption, underwater earthquakes created giant tidal waves called **tsunamis**. Tsunamis flooded the land for 8,000 miles (12,875 km) around Krakatoa. People did not have time to run for cover. Krakatoa destroyed 165 villages in Indonesia and damaged another 132 villages.

The tsunamis created by Krakatoa were thought to be as tall as 99 feet (30 m) high. That's about as high as a 10-story building!

The eruption caused beautiful sunsets, like this sunset over Indonesia.

Krakatoa Sunsets

The 1883 eruption of Krakatoa was a reminder of how terrible nature can be. It was also a reminder of nature's beauty. The dust and ash from the eruption traveled 17 miles (27.4 km) into the sky. Wind carried the dust all the way around Earth for two years. During this time, the dust blocked some of the sun's light, which made the moon and the sun appear to turn blue, then green, then even pink! People all around the world saw amazing sunsets and sunrises because of the dust. It was beautiful, but it was also cold. The volcanic dust was blocking the sun's rays. This meant that the weather everywhere was colder than usual for the two years that the dust was in the air.

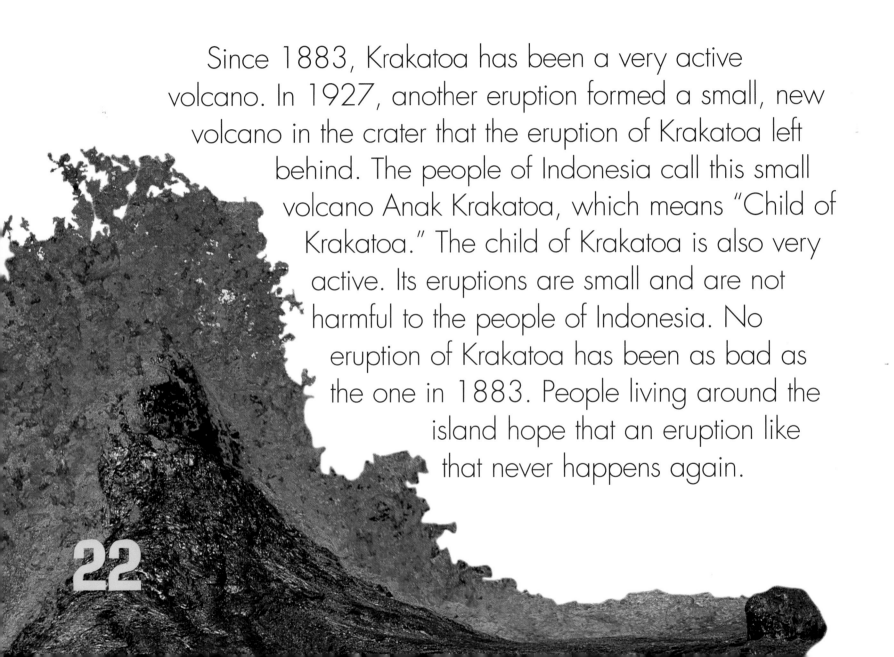

Child of Krakatoa

Since 1883, Krakatoa has been a very active volcano. In 1927, another eruption formed a small, new volcano in the crater that the eruption of Krakatoa left behind. The people of Indonesia call this small volcano Anak Krakatoa, which means "Child of Krakatoa." The child of Krakatoa is also very active. Its eruptions are small and are not harmful to the people of Indonesia. No eruption of Krakatoa has been as bad as the one in 1883. People living around the island hope that an eruption like that never happens again.

Glossary

ash (ASH) Tiny pieces of rock that shoot out of a volcano during an eruption.

caldera (kal-DEHR-ah) A crater formed by a volcano.

core (KOHR) The hot center layer of Earth that is made of liquid and solid iron and other elements.

crater (KRAY-ter) A hole in the ground that is shaped like a bowl.

crust (KRUST) The top layer of Earth where we live.

earthquake (URTH-kwayk) A movement or shaking of Earth.

erupted (ih-RUP-ted) Having had an eruption, which is an explosion of gases, smoke, or lava from a volcano.

gases (GAS-ez) Matter that has no shape or size.

lava (LAH-va) Magma that has reached Earth's crust.

magma (MAG-mah) Hot liquid rock found in the mantle of Earth.

mantle (MAN-tuhl) The middle layer of Earth, made of solid rock and magma.

plates (PLAYTZ) Large sections of Earth's crust that move and shift over time.

submarine volcano (sub-mahr-EEHN vohl-KAYH-noh) A volcano that begins on the ocean floor.

tsunamis (soo-NAH-meez) A series of waves caused by a disturbance in Earth's crust in or near the ocean.

23

Index

A
Anak Krakatoa, 22
ash, 14, 21

C
caldera, 17
core, 6
crater, 17, 22
crust, 6

D
dust, 14, 21

E
earthquake, 13, 18
eruption, 10, 13, 14, 17,
    18, 21, 22
explosion, 5, 18

G
gases, 14

L
lava, 6, 9, 10, 17

M
magma, 6
mantle, 6

S
submarine volcano, 9
sunsets, 21

T
tsunamis, 18

Web Sites

To learn more about volcanoes and Krakatoa, check out these Web sites:
http://volcano.und.nodak.edu/vwdocs/volc_images
/southeast_asia/indonesia/krakatau.html
http://www.irfamedia.com/lampung/krakatau.htm

24